Spice It Up!

Contents

Features

Long before Europeans discovered the Spice Islands, the Bugis sailed to and from the islands. Discover more in **Pirates or Traders?** on page 13.

Do you speak clearly? Test how well your tongue twists, and spice up your vocabulary on page 15.

What gift would you treasure if you were getting married? Find out what spicy gift Indian brides were once given on page 19.

Follow the steps to make a delicious and nutritious spicy meal in a glass in **Make a Vanilla-Banana Smoothie** on page 23.

How do people make curry powder?
Visit www.rigbyinfoquest.com
for more about SPICES.

The Spice of Life

Fortunes have been made and nations discovered because of spices. The vibrant colors, inviting smells, and exciting flavors of herbs and spices have been favorite ingredients in kitchens around the world for thousands of years.

Today, when herbs and spices cost so little, we can travel the world in our imagination while enjoying the vast variety of tastes and **aromas** of faraway lands.

Root

Bark

Flowers

Seed pods

Seeds

Leaves

IN FOCUS

Herbs and spices are fresh or dried parts of a plant. Spices generally grow in hot countries. They come from the bark, flowers, roots, and seeds of plants.

Today, many of the spices we buy have been ground into a fine powder. Sometimes, spices such as cinnamon can be bought dried but not yet ground. A spice has a fresher flavor if it is ground as it is needed. The illustration on the title page shows a traditional spice grinder found in many kitchens in India.

Herbs usually come from the leaves of plants and are best used fresh. They grow in **temperate** climates.

Spice and Mystery

In ancient times, herbs and spices were rare and precious products. For centuries, Arabs controlled the trade of spices, which came mainly from the **Far East**. The Arab traders kept their sources of supply a secret. They told tales of the dangers they faced in far-off lands to frighten away other traders.

The busy market of Baghdad was an important meeting place for traders from Asia and Europe. Spice traders brought pepper and cloves from India, cinnamon and nutmeg from Indonesia, and ginger from China.

The ancient Persian Empire stretched as far as Egypt and India and included Baghdad in what is now Iraq.

In the Baghdad market, traders would spend hours talking before agreeing on the best price for goods they were buying or selling.

In the days before refrigeration, spices were used to disguise the taste of old meat. They were also used to make **incense,** perfume, and medicine.

Arab traders sailed
in ships called dhows.
Today, many dhows
are still built in the
same way they were
hundreds of years ago.

Arab Trading Routes

EUROPE

Baghdad

PERSIA

EGYPT

AFRICA

INDIA

ASIA

CHINA

INDIAN OCEAN

INDONESIA

The Pepper Hunt

In medieval times, Italy controlled the Mediterranean Sea and trade with Asia. The spice trade flowed through the Italian ports to the rest of Europe. Pepper was the largest import and was in high demand. The Italian traders demanded high prices.

Other European countries began searching for new routes to the spice-producing lands. They wanted to break the **monopoly** of the Italian traders. The hunt for pepper led to some of the greatest sea adventures in history.

In 1497, the Portuguese sailor Vasco da Gama rounded the Cape of Good Hope, and he arrived in India in 1498. Spice traders were shocked to see the Portuguese ships and realized that their monopoly was now broken. Vasco da Gama returned to Portugal with his ships filled with pepper, cinnamon, ginger, and jewels. Europe realized that spice-producing lands could be reached by more than one sea route, and the race to dominate the valuable spice business began.

Vasco da Gama

EUROPE

PORTUGAL   ITALY

ATLANTIC
OCEAN

PERSIA

ARABIA   INDIA

AFRICA

INDIAN OCEAN

Cape of Good Hope

**Vasco da Gama's
Route to India**

The Spice Race

From the 1500s through the late 1700s, Spain, Portugal, England, and Holland all fought for control of the spice trade. Ferdinand Magellan's **circumnavigation** of Earth was Spain's attempt to find a shorter route to the Spice Islands in Southeast Asia.

In 1600, Queen Elizabeth I of England set up the British East India Company and began to take control of India. By the late 1600s, Holland had taken control of many of the Spice Islands. In 1780, the Dutch and English fought a war over the spice trade that destroyed Holland's power in the East.

The Dutch were determined to control the spice trade and fiercely protected entry into their islands. The French managed to get enough nutmeg (shown left), clove, and cinnamon plants to begin growing spices in the French islands of the Indian Ocean and in French Guinea on the northern coast of South America.

In the 1500s and 1600s, the country with the strongest navy was often able to control the countries where spices were grown. British navigators, such as Sir Francis Drake (shown presenting a pearl necklace to Queen Elizabeth I), and the British navy's defeat of the Spanish Armada in 1588 made Britain a power at sea.

Islands of Spice

For thousands of years before European explorers arrived in Southeast Asia, the adventurous Bugis people were the masters of the sea. The Bugis built and sailed ships to carry spices and cargo to and from the 13,000 islands in the region. They traded with Arab and Chinese merchants, who then started their journeys to the markets of Europe and China.

Islands of Southeast Asia

- SINGAPORE
- SUMATRA
- JAVA
- SULAWESI
- MOLUCCAS
- NEW GUINEA

CHINA

INDIA

INDONESIA

AUSTRALIA

The Bugis came from an island called Sulawesi. Close to Sulawesi are the Molucca Islands. The Moluccas were known as the Spice Islands and were famous for the cloves and nutmeg that grew there. The Moluccas and Sulawesi are now part of Indonesia.

When the Dutch arrived in the region, they cut off the traditional Bugis spice trade from Sulawesi to Java, and they forced the Bugis to migrate to other areas. The Dutch introduced new crops such as tea, coffee, sugar, and tobacco.

TIME LINK

Pirates or Traders?

The Dutch fought to break the Bugis' trading links. They feared the Bugis sailors and called them pirates.

Today, a large community of Bugis live in Singapore, where many moved after violent disagreements with the Dutch in the early 1800s.

Bugis sailors continue to sail the seas from Singapore and Sumatra to the Moluccas and New Guinea. Their boats sail to tiny island ports and large mainland cities.

Picking tea in Java

13

Hot! Hot! Hot!

Pepper Confusion

No one is really sure where the hottest spice, chili, originally came from. Some people think the chili first grew in the Amazon jungles. Seeds, carried by the river and later by Aztec Indians, spread throughout South and Central America and up to Mexico.

In 1492, six years before Vasco da Gama reached the East, Christopher Columbus set sail. He was hoping to find a direct western route to the Far East and to the home of pepper. Instead, he arrived in the Americas. The closest thing he could find to pepper was the chili. Columbus called the fiery vegetable "red pepper." Confusion over the use of the word *pepper* continues today.

Chili market in Nigeria

Peter Piper picked a peck of pickled peppers.

WORD BUILDER

This tongue-twisting rhyme is often used to practice clear speech. When a letter or sound at the beginning of a word is repeated in words close to each other, it is called alliteration. See if you can use alliteration to make a rhyme about another spice.

A peck is a unit of measure for foods such as spices, grains, fruits, and vegetables. One peck equals eight quarts. Peter picked a lot of peppers!

HOT CHILIES

15

Cowboys, Mexicans, and Chili

If you think of Mexican food, your tongue may tingle and your eyes may water. Mexican food can be hot! Hispanic people use chilies in many different foods. They use them roasted, stewed, fried, or simply fresh from the plant. There are more than 2,000 different varieties of the chili pepper, and they come in a wide range of colors, sizes, shapes, and spiciness.

Mexican food was influenced when the Spanish colonists introduced spices and foods from Africa, South America, the Caribbean, France, and the East to Mexico. Today, a new **cuisine** known as Tex-Mex has become popular. It combines Mexican flavors with traditional Texan cowboy food. Chili is an important ingredient in many Tex-Mex recipes.

A tradition in New Mexico is to tie red chilies together into colorful long strings known as *ristras.* The *ristras* are hung near the entrances of homes as a symbol of friendliness.

Texans take their chilies very seriously! Every year, "chili cook-offs" are held to find the best recipes using chilies. Some say that the secret to a successful pot of chili is to use a lot of very hot chili peppers.

In the early 1800s, English settlers in Texas ground together dried garlic, chili peppers, and oregano while trying to make a dish similar to the curries they had in their homeland. Thus, ground chili powder was invented. The early settlers could now make almost anything taste hot and spicy.

A Taste of India

The surprising colors, flavors, aromas, and feel of the food of India help to show the many different ways that history and culture have shaped the nation. The different traditional and religious communities within India each have their own special cuisine. They use spices and prepare food in various ways.

Only a handful of spices are, in fact, native to India. These include cardamom, kari leaf, and pepper. Some spices, such as saffron, were introduced to India by Persian traders over 4,000 years ago. Other herbs and spices were introduced over the centuries by immigrants. The ancient Romans brought coriander, cumin, and fennel, and the Portuguese brought chilies.

Long ago, when a girl in an Indian village married, she was given a *masaladani*, or spice box. The covered container had several compartments containing spices for the bride to take to her new family and new home. Some boxes were carved from wood, while others were made of gold and decorated with precious jewels.

Costly Spices

Threads of Saffron

Luckily, the tiniest amount of saffron goes a long way. This is fortunate because it is the world's most expensive spice. Saffron is made from the **stigmas**, or threads, of the violet-colored saffron flower. Each saffron flower has three delicate stigmas. It takes about 14,000 hand-picked stigmas to make just 1 ounce of the deep orange spice!

Saffron has been harvested for thousands of years. Its delicate flavor and strong color are in many Mediterranean and Asian dishes.

Only half a teaspoon of saffron threads have been used to give this rice a rich yellow color. Cinnamon, cloves, and cardamom pods are other spices that add flavor to this classic Indian dish called *Kesar Bhat*.

Stigmas, or threads

In India, farmers **cultivate** fields of saffron flowers. Saffron is grown in many places, including Spain, Turkey, China, and Iran.

Stigma

Saffron flowers

Beans of Vanilla

Mmm . . . vanilla. Its aroma brings thoughts of delicious ice creams, cakes, cookies, and pies. Vanilla is the fruit of a type of **orchid** plant, and it grows in the form of a bean pod. Inside each bean are thousands of tiny, black seeds.

Spanish explorers discovered vanilla in Mexico and brought it back to Europe, where it quickly became popular. Vanilla orchids now grow in many other tropical countries. As with saffron, the production of vanilla is complicated, making it expensive. Also, like saffron, a small amount has a large effect.

Vanilla pod

Make a Vanilla-Banana Smoothie

This quick and easy drink not only tastes great but also gives you lots of energy.

TRY THIS!

You Will Need:

- 1 cup orange juice
- 1 cup plain yogurt
- 1 medium banana, peeled and sliced
- 1 teaspoon vanilla extract (pure or imitation)

Method:

Have an adult help you blend all the ingredients until they're smooth. Makes two drinks.

Variations:

Add 1/2 cup fruit such as blueberries or strawberries. Sprinkle a pinch of nutmeg or cinnamon on top for an extra-sweet flavor.

Using vanilla beans, or pods, in food preparation can be time consuming. Liquid vanilla extract, commercially produced from the beans, is used instead. Imitation vanilla extract is also available. It is cheaper but has a similar flavor.

Salt and Pepper

Today, salt and pepper are readily available, and many people add them to their food. In ancient times, salt and pepper were both very precious and sometimes exchanged for other goods. Salt was often traded for the same weight in gold. In many areas around the Mediterranean Sea, cakes of salt were used for **currency.**

In ancient times, salt was produced in the center of the Sahara, the largest desert in the world. Traders used camel caravans to carry heavy loads of salt to West Africa, where the salt was traded for gold and other goods.

Pepper was a very popular and valuable spice in the Roman Empire. A single peppercorn dropped on the floor was hunted like a lost pearl. The main street on Rome's spice market was called *Via Piperatica,* Latin for "Pepper Street." When the Roman Empire fell, the supply of pepper and many other spices dried up in Europe.

TIME LINK

The first salt and pepper shakers were made in the 1860s. Early shakers were really mills. Salt came in rock form, and mills ground the salt and peppercorns into pieces. Salt and pepper shakers became popular in the 1940s when it became easier to make a variety of shapes and designs.

Pepper

Salt

Mountains of Salt

Salt is necessary to both life and taste. A small amount of salt is important in our diet. Salt also brings out the flavor in food. Without it, food can taste **bland.** Since ancient times, salt has been used for preserving food. Today, salt is mainly used in the chemical industry for manufacturing such products as glass, paper, pesticides, antifreeze, and soap. It is also often spread on roads to melt snow and ice.

The coastline of Vietnam is dotted with evaporation ponds and mountains of salt. China, France, India, Italy, Japan, and Spain also produce solar salt.

Most salt comes from salt mines and the sea. Rock salt is mined from underground deposits formed by the evaporation of oceans millions of years ago. Solar salt is formed by evaporating seawater. This is the oldest method of harvesting salt and requires a hot, dry climate.

WORD BUILDER

Salt **seasons** language as well as food. A person described as "the salt of the Earth" is seen as being honest and hardworking. To "take it with a grain of salt" means don't believe everything you are told because some of it may not be true. To "rub salt into the wound" means to make a situation worse. To "salt away" your money means to save a little money regularly.

Underground salt deposits are found on every continent. Most of the salt mined in Canada comes from underground deposits in the southwestern provinces of Canada. In winter months, Canadians use large quantities of salt to melt snow on the roads.

Fields of Color

Mustard is one of the oldest spices and is one of the world's most popular seasonings. The Chinese have grown mustard for 3,000 years. Ancient Egyptians popped mustard seeds into their mouths while chewing meat. The ancient Greeks and Romans used it as an everyday spice to flavor food.

Dijon, France, has been an important center for mustard production since the 1200s. The French consider mustard the **condiment** of kings. Dijon mustard is made from ground mustard seeds, blended with vinegar, cloves, cinnamon, and other herbs and spices.

There are many ready-made mustards, flavored from mild and sweet to sharp and strong. The smooth mustard sauce often added to hot dogs is made from mustard seeds blended with sugar, vinegar, and the yellow spice turmeric.

A girl harvests mustard seeds from a field covered with golden blooms. In India, mustard seeds are used as a **garnish** and for seasoning. The seeds are also ground with other spices to make curry powders and paste. Oil from mustard seeds is used in cooking.

SITESEEING · PEOPLE & PLACES ·

How do people make curry powder?
Visit **www.rigbyinfoquest.com**
for more about SPICES.

Glossary

aroma – a smell that is usually pleasant

bland – mild and rather dull, or plain in flavor

circumnavigation – sailing all the way around

condiment – a substance that is used to add flavor to food. Herbs and spices are condiments.

cuisine – a style or way of cooking or presenting food

cultivate – to grow and care for plants

currency – the money used in a country

Far East – the countries of east Asia, including Indonesia, Malaysia, Singapore, Vietnam, China, and Japan

garnish – to decorate food with small amounts of other food, herbs, or spices to make it look or taste better

incense – a substance that gives off a sweet smell when it is burned

monopoly – complete control of a service or product in some place by a single person or company. A company that has a monopoly has no competition.

orchid – a plant with colorful and unusually shaped flowers

season – add to or change the flavor of food with herbs, salt, or spices

stigma – the part of a flower that receives pollen during pollination

temperate – a climate that is neither very hot nor very cold. The United States, southern Australia, and New Zealand all have temperate climates.

Index

Research Starters

1 There are many different spices in the world. Think of a spice not described in this book and research its history. Where does it grow today? How is it used with food? Does it have other uses?

2 Choose a country, not your own, that grows and exports spices. Locate the country on a map of the world. Find out about other products that this country exports. What is the population of the country and what languages do the people speak? What other interesting facts about this country can you find?

3 Interview an adult you know who enjoys cooking. Which herbs and spices does the person use? Does the person have a favorite herb or spice? Why? In which recipe is this herb or spice used?

4 Find out all you can about the history of serving salt and pepper and the materials used to make shakers. Design a set of shakers unlike any you've seen.